What Lies Within

Understanding the Holy Spirit

Robert R. Davis

I0202472

What Lies Within

Understanding the Holy Spirit

Robert R. Davis

Kingdom Works Publishing

What Lies Within
Understanding the Holy Spirit
© Copyright 2010, Robert R. Davis

All rights reserved. No part of this book may be reproduced, stored in a retrieval system, or transmitted by any means, electronic, mechanical, photocopying, recording, or otherwise – except for brief quotations in printed reviews, without written permission from the author.

All scripture quotations, unless otherwise indicated, are taken from the Holy Bible (King James Version) 1.42.01. Copyright © 1992-2004 by Timnathserah Inc. Used by permission of Online Bible, www.OnlineBible.org. All rights reserved. The author has inserted italics and bolding used in quotations from Scripture.

To order this or other Kingdom Works Publishing books. For more information or to contact the author, visit our website at **http://www.kingdomworkspublishing.com**. The publisher offers discounts on this book when ordered in quantity.

Contents

Chapter 1

Who is the Holy Spirit

If ye then, being evil, know how to give good gifts
unto your children: how much more shall your
heavenly Father give the Holy Spirit to them that
ask him?

St. Luke 11:13

We were created in the image and likeness of God or to be more exact the Godhead. Yet we have little understanding of the Trinity. How can God be, the Father, the Son and the Holy Ghost? Although the word Trinity is not mentioned in the Bible, we know God is three in one (1 John 5:7). There are three very distinct personifications that make up the Godhead and they are equal in authority.

Today we understand God the Father and Jesus the Son as two very distinct entities within the Godhead. However, there has been much confusion over the identity of the Holy Spirit. Many people throughout the ages have thought of the Holy Spirit more as a thing than a Person. To get a better understanding of the Holy Ghost we should look at the physical representation of the Godhead, humans.

God the Father's number in the trinity is one, the Son is two, and the Spirit is three. Six is the numerical representation of man. **Genesis declares, man was created in the image of the Godhead, in their image and in their likeness.** This truth is confirmed in words and numbers.

$$1 + 2 + 3 = 6$$
Father + Son + Holy Ghost = Man (Image of the Godhead)

It is almost a universally accepted fact that man is a triune being, composed of body, soul and spirit. Since we were made in the likeness and image of the Godhead, the trinity of man should resemble the Trinity of God. God the Father is the head of Christ (1 Corinthians 11:3) and the Trinity (1 Corinthians 15:28). Therefore, the mind or soul of man is the best match to the role of the Father. Jesus the Son of God is the visible part of the Trinity. Therefore, our corporeal bodies are the best representation of the Son. By default the Holy Spirit corresponds to our spirit.

Father	Mind (Soul)
Son	Body
Holy Spirit	Spirit

The natural things help us understand the spiritual. The Old Testament with all of its ceremonies and rituals is given to help us understand the spiritual realities of our salvation. This is why the physical things of God precede the spiritual, so that we may understand them.

> *1 Corinthians 15:46 Howbeit that was not first which is spiritual, but that which is natural; and afterward that which is spiritual.*

Since the physical or natural helps us understand the spiritual, we should look at ourselves in order to better comprehend the Trinity. Although humans have three distinct parts, mind, body and spirit, they are considered one person. Likewise, God is made up of three distinct parts, Father, Son and Holy Spirit, yet they are also considered one deity. In people the body is easily distinguishable from the soul and the spirit. The same is true of God. Jesus is easily perceptible from the Father and the Spirit. There is no clear distinction between the soul and spirit of man, the two are tightly intertwined. Likewise the Father and the Spirit are so tightly bound they are practically indistinguishable.

Jesus is the Son of God, but it was the Holy Spirit that overshadowed (impregnated) Mary. Jesus, however, is not considered the Son of the Holy Ghost but of the Father (St. Luke 1:35). This shows how intricate and fused God and the Holy Spirit are in their nature. So, when we are filled with the Spirit, we have God the Father within. There is no difference between being filled with the Spirit and being filled with the Father.

Likewise, Christ and the Father are one. Jesus said to Philip, "Don't you know me, even after I have been among you such a long time? How can you say, show us the Father?"[1] Therefore, with a little deductive reasoning we can surmise that if we have one part of the Trinity, we have all of it.

Fact 1: God the Father = Holy Spirit
Fact 2: Christ = God the Father
Conclusion: God the Father = Christ = Holy Ghost

Deductive reasoning also leads us to the conclusion that Christ is equal to Holy Ghost, given facts one and two.

> So, when someone is filled with the Holy Spirit they are in fact filled with the Father, Son and Holy Ghost.

There are some who believe that the Holy Spirit is feminine, or has feminine aspects. Based on the genders of the verbs in the original Bible languages where the Holy Spirit is the subject. In Hebrew the word for spirit (*ruach*) is feminine. In Greek the word (*pneuma*) is neuter, and in Aramaic, the language which is generally considered to have been spoken by Jesus, the word is feminine. This is not thought by most linguists to have significance for the gender of the *person* given that name. There are biblical cases where the pronoun used for the Holy Spirit is masculine, in contradiction of the gender of the word for *spirit* (John 16:13).[2]

We can safely conclude that God the Father and Jesus the Son are male. We know that the three are one. Can one of the three parts be considered feminine and the others masculine? That is doubtful. Earlier we saw it was the Holy Spirit, which impregnated Mary. This act implies the Holy Ghost is also masculine. Therefore, there are no feminine aspects to the Godhead or Trinity.

> There are no feminine aspects to the Godhead or Trinity

Popular literature started claiming the Church was suppressing the *Sacred Feminine*, referring to the representation of the mystical power of the earth or mother goddess. Some point to either Mary Magdalene or the Madonna (Mary the mother of Jesus) as the object of adoration. **The true faith has no worship of a female deity because New Jerusalem is the bride of Christ and the mother of us all.** As Christians we makeup New Jerusalem, it is not something outside ourselves. So, the feminine element is neither absent nor suppressed, we just failed to comprehend the Church's role in the Godhead.

When the Bible speaks of God being masculine, He is personifying Himself in order for us to better understand Him. God uses gender in the Bible to convey object lessons to us. In the same manner the various names of the Spirit serve to communicate different aspects of His nature.

The Old Testament term for Spirit is the Hebrew word "*ruach*" (pronounced roo'-akh) which means wind, even the wind associated with a breath. The New Testament expression for Spirit is the Greek word "pneuma" (pronounced pnyoo'-mah) which also means breath or breeze. **The implication is the Holy Spirit is literally the breath of God.** This means that the Holy Ghost is the life force of God. That is why He is seen throughout creation, the birth of Jesus and His resurrection. But, the Spirit is more than a force that gives life. The Holy Spirit is the very essence or nature of God. This is why we can call God our Father and not just our creator. He has placed His nature inside of us via His Spirit.

The Holy Spirit is the very essence or nature of God

The Holy Spirit is the Spirit of God. It is the heart so to speak of God, which has been breathed into us. He is the essence, life and nature of God in us. Now that we know who the Holy Spirit is, we can begin to look at His purpose.

Chapter 2

The Purpose of the Holy Spirit

Know ye not that ye are the temple of God, and that the Spirit of God dwelleth in you?

1 Corinthians 3:16

The full purpose of the Holy Spirit is too manifold for the scope of this work. I will address just some of the major purposes of the Spirit as they relate to the believer and the Church. One of the best ways to discover the Spirit's purpose is through His various names and symbols. For brevity sake I will list just a few purposes of the Holy Ghost.

The Comforter:

Jesus referred to the Holy Ghost as the Comforter to the disciples. Christ was about to go to the cross and His followers would sorely miss Him. Jesus declared in the book of St. Matthew He would always be with them, even to the end of the world.[3] Physically this was not feasible, but through the Holy Spirit He could keep this promise.

The Holy Ghost will abide in believers until the end of the earth. This should bring comfort to all who follow the Lord.

> *St. John 14:26 But the Comforter, which is the Holy Ghost, whom the Father will send in my name, he shall teach you all things, and bring all things to your remembrance, whatsoever I have said unto you.*

To teach us:

Christ declared the Holy Spirit would teach us all things. What things? Jesus told us everything already, right?

> *St. John 16:12* ***I have yet many things to say unto you, but ye cannot bear them now.***

Jesus said that He had many things to say before He was crucified, but the disciples could not bear them at that point. So, the Holy Ghost was commissioned to speak to the Church after Jesus' death and continue where He left off, not only that, but the Spirit will also bring everything Jesus taught to our remembrance.

Some people are very "by the book" and if it is not in the Bible, then it is not of God, end of story. This attitude is not conducive to allowing the Spirit of God full course in our lives. We are supposed to try or test the spirits to see if it is from God (the Holy Spirit). How do we test the spirit?

> *1 John 4:1* ***Beloved, believe not every spirit, but try the spirits whether they are of God****: because many false prophets are gone out into the world.*

We test the spirits by comparing what we hear, against what is written in the Bible. The Holy Ghost will never contradict the Word, but He will fill in the blanks and give us a fuller understanding of what has been written.

Testifies of Christ:

The Spirit testifies by convicting the hearers concerning the truth of the Gospel. The Holy Ghost convinces the hearer of sin in their life, He pricks our heart so to speak.

The Spirit also testifies by performing signs and wonders. When healings and miracles follow the spoken Word, this is done to testify that it is of God.

> *St. John 15:26 But when the Comforter is come, whom I will send unto you from the Father, even the* ***Spirit of truth, which proceedeth from the Father, he shall testify of me****:*
> *St. John 15:27 And ye also shall bear witness, because ye have been with me from the beginning.*

Spirit of Life:

The Spirit is also called the Breath of Life. This means that the Holy Spirit is the life force of God. He is seen throughout creation, the birth of Jesus and the resurrection of Christ. Through the Spirit we have eternal life.

> *Romans 8:10 And if Christ be in you, the body is dead because of sin; but* ***the Spirit is life*** *because of righteousness.*

Romans 8:11 But if the Spirit of him that raised up
Jesus from the dead dwell in you, he that raised up
*Christ from the dead **shall also quicken your***
mortal bodies by his Spirit that dwelleth in you.

Spirit of Adoption:

The Holy Spirit is the very essence or nature of God. This
is why we can call God our Father and not just our creator.
We are no longer the servants of God, but we are His
children. This is part of the better covenant, which is based
on better promises.

Romans 8:14 For as many as are led by the Spirit
of God, they are the sons of God.
Romans 8:15 For ye have not received the spirit of
*bondage again to fear; but **ye have received the***
Spirit of adoption, whereby we cry, Abba, Father.
Romans 8:16 The Spirit itself beareth witness with
our spirit, that we are the children of God:

Spirit of Promise:

Every believer has been sealed with the Holy Spirit of
Promise. This name informs us that we are still waiting on
God to complete our redemption. Presently, our spirits
have been regenerated to house the Holy Ghost and our
souls have experienced redemption from death, but our
bodies are still awaiting the resurrection power of Christ.

Ephesians 1:13 In whom ye also trusted, after that
ye heard the word of truth, the gospel of your
*salvation: in whom also after that ye believed, **ye***
were sealed with that holy Spirit of promise,

*Ephesians 1:14 Which is the earnest of our
inheritance until the redemption of the purchased
possession, unto the praise of his glory.*

Empowers us to be Witnesses:

The apostles and disciples who walked with Jesus, had to
wait for the Holy Spirit to come upon them before they
could be witnesses. A witness is someone who has
personal knowledge of something. Why did they need the
Holy Ghost to be witnesses?

God wanted the disciples to do more than repeat what they
saw Jesus do. He wanted them to do what He did. Another
definition of a witness is something (someone) serving as
evidence, proof or a sign. They needed the power of the
Spirit, in order to be living proof that Jesus was God. This
is not only the signs and wonders, but more importantly
being able to live transformed lives through the Spirit of
Holiness.

We are poor witnesses of Christ, if our lives are not a
personal demonstration of His saving power.   Every
believer is called to be a witness of Christ.

> *Acts 1:8 But **ye shall receive power, after that the
> Holy Ghost is come upon you: and ye shall be
> witnesses unto me** both in Jerusalem, and in all
> Judaea, and in Samaria, and unto the uttermost part
> of the earth.*

Living Water:

Water is a ubiquitous chemical substance that is composed

of hydrogen and oxygen and is essential for all known forms of life. Likewise, the Spirit of God is omnipresent and absolutely essential to all known forms of life, especially humans.

> *St. John 4:14 But **whosoever drinketh of the water that I shall give him shall never thirst**; but the water that I shall give him shall be in him a well of water springing up into everlasting life.*

The Anointing:

The Holy Ghost anoints believers to commission them into service for God. We are the priests of the New Testament dispensation. Through Christ we have been made into a kingdom of priests. As priests we have the authority to administer religious rites and to restore people back to God.

> *Revelation 1:4 **John, To the seven churches** in the province of Asia: Grace and peace to you from him who is, and who was, and who is to come, and from the seven spirits before his throne,*
> *Revelation 1:5 and from Jesus Christ, who is the faithful witness, the firstborn from the dead, and the ruler of the kings of the earth. **To him who loves us and has freed us from our sins by his blood,***
> *Revelation 1:6 **and has made us to be a kingdom and priests to serve his God and Father**—to him be glory and power for ever and ever! Amen. (NIV)*

Chapter 3

Receiving the Holy Spirit

And when he had said this, he breathed on them,
and saith unto them, Receive ye the Holy Ghost:
St. John 20:22

Before we can talk about receiving the Holy Ghost, we must address the baptism of the Holy Spirit. Why? The baptism of the Spirit always precedes His indwelling.

The baptism of the Holy Spirit was instituted and performed by Jesus. He is the one who baptizes us in the fire of the Holy Ghost. Christ never physically baptized anyone during His First Advent because the baptism He administers is the Holy Spirit. This is done automatically upon salvation.

St. John 4:1 When therefore the Lord knew how the Pharisees had heard that Jesus made and baptized more disciples than John,
*St. John 4:2 (**Though Jesus himself baptized not, but his disciples,**)*

When you receive Christ, the Spirit is automatically regenerated (reborn) within you. To regenerate means to form or create again. The baptism of the Holy Ghost, which is synonymous with regeneration, restores the temple structure within man's spirit.

Baptism is symbolic of death and resurrection. Ordinarily, water is the symbol for baptism but fire is the conduit for the Holy Spirit. Why? The point that is being conveyed by water is simply death. Water is being used symbolically as the grave. The illustration of baptism by fire speaks of not simply death but a sacrifice unto God.

The baptism of the Holy Ghost points to our death and resurrection in Christ. Furthermore, it says we have wholly dedicated ourselves to God as a burnt offering upon His altar. This death upon the altar is voluntary; we present ourselves to God that we may be totally dedicated and well pleasing to Him. The fire of the Holy Ghost is an explicit reference to the fact of our death.

The baptism of the Spirit mimics the sacrifice of Christ. He voluntarily sacrificed His life for us and became our salvation. When we accept Him, we are willingly sacrificing ourselves to God in reaction to Christ's work. This is a response of love. We freely crucify the flesh in order to live for the Lord. The death we die is to our flesh or self; now, we wholly dedicate our lives and our will to God.

Baptism and infilling of the Holy Spirit, are two separate things. The baptism of the Holy Ghost is the rebuilding of the temple, and the infilling with the Holy Ghost is the habitation of God within man. First, the temple must be rebuilt via regeneration (baptism); then, God can inhabit the building via the outpouring of His Spirit. Observe carefully the wording and sequence of the scriptures.

First the Baptism

*Acts 2:3 And **there appeared unto them cloven tongues like as of fire, and it sat upon each of them.***

Afterward the Infilling

*Acts 2:4 **And they were all filled with the Holy Ghost**, and began to speak with other tongues, as the Spirit gave them utterance.*

Notice on the day of Pentecost the first thing that happened is that the tongues of fire sat or rested on them. This picture is alluding to the disciples being purified, like a sacrifice (burnt offering) by the fire of the Holy Spirit. Then, afterward, they were all filled with the Holy Ghost and began to speak with other tongues. The filling of the Spirit means to receive the power of God because through this act God himself resides within us. So, first the temple is rebuilt and cleansed, then God can dwell in it (St. John 14:23).

In practical terms, if you want a glass of water, the first thing you would do is ensure the glass is clean. So, the glass must first be washed (immersed) in water, but this water is for cleaning not drinking. After the glass is thoroughly cleaned, it is filled with water to drink. So, water in this example has two distinct functions. The same is true spiritually. We must first be baptized (immersed) by the Holy Ghost, but this work of the Spirit is for cleaning, not filling. After we are thoroughly cleaned, we are ready to be filled with the Holy Spirit. Like the water, the Holy Ghost has two distinct functions.

Baptism of the Holy Spirit prepares us. Infilling of the Holy Spirit equips us.

Baptism and infilling can occur together like the day of Pentecost or can be separate events. You can be baptized with the Spirit and after a week or more be filled with the Spirit. Again, think about it in terms of the natural. You can wash a glass in water one day and not fill the glass with water to drink for a week or more. It does not matter if the two acts happen together or separately. What is important to note is the washing (baptism) always precedes the filling, in the natural and in the spiritual.

How does someone get filled with the Holy Ghost? Laying on of hands is the prescribed means to receiving the Holy Spirit. We can receive it on our own through faith, but the ministry is commissioned to impart the Holy Ghost. The Church has this ministry because it stands in Christ's stead. Can the laity or every believer administer the Holy Spirit? There is no precedent for it, and there is no prohibition against it. In the New Testament we only see the laying on of hands for the Holy Spirit administered by Church leaders. Since traditionally this act is performed by the ministry, I would advise that lay members consult with their own churches.

Some in the Church tarry for the Holy Ghost. To tarry means to wait. The apostles were told to tarry at Jerusalem for the initial outpouring of the Spirit, but after that we do not see anyone tarrying for the Holy Ghost again. What we do see is the apostles laying hands on anyone who wants to receive God's Spirit. We also see Gentiles receiving the Spirit without the laying of hands in order to demonstrate to the apostles that God is not a respecter of persons. Nowhere after Pentecost do we find believers waiting for the Holy

Ghost to fall on them. The promise of the Spirit has been fulfilled and we no longer have to tarry to receive it.

The laying on of hands for the Holy Ghost works like healing. The recipient receives it through faith. Whether the evidence is present or not, receivers must believe they have it through faith. Just as you thank God and claim your healing, you must thank God for the Holy Ghost and claim it (St. Mark 11:23–24).

Faith is the foundation to obtain anything from God. Therefore, receiving the Holy Ghost is an act of faith. In order to be filled with the Spirit we must have faith. If we do not have the evidence of the Spirit, then we need to continue in faith until we have the manifestation. This is the pattern for how we receive everything in the spirit realm. The spiritual reality of faith is that we have it now, but the physical manifestation is sometimes delayed.

What is the manifestation of the Spirit? There are two signs of the indwelling of the Holy Ghost, one is prophesying and the other is speaking in tongues. This is liable to be an issue of controversy, because some believe that tongues are not necessary to be filled. Therefore, we should look at the scriptures for guidance on the subject.

> *Numbers 11:24 And Moses went out, and told the people the words of the LORD, and gathered the seventy men of the elders of the people, and set them round about the tabernacle.*
> *Numbers 11:25 And **the LORD** came down in a cloud, and spake unto him, and **took of the spirit that was upon him, and gave it unto the seventy elders:** and it came to pass, that, **when the spirit rested upon them, they prophesied, and did not cease.***

Numbers 11:26 **But there remained two of the men in the camp, the name of the one was Eldad, and the name of the other Medad: and the spirit rested upon them;** *and they were of them that were written, but went not out unto the tabernacle: and* **they prophesied in the camp.**
Numbers 11:27 And there ran a young man, and told Moses, and said, Eldad and Medad do prophesy in the camp.
Numbers 11:28 And Joshua the son of Nun, the servant of Moses, one of his young men, answered and said, My lord Moses, forbid them.
Numbers 11:29 And Moses said unto him, Enviest thou for my sake? would God that all the LORD'S people were prophets, and that the LORD would put his spirit upon them!

1st Witness

In the book of Numbers, we see that Moses needed help leading the multitude (Israel). So, God took the Spirit that was on Moses and gave it to seventy elders. When the Spirit rested on the elders, they immediately began to prophesy. Two of the seventy do not go to the tabernacle as instructed, Eldad and Medad. But, the Spirit rested on them also and they began to prophesy in the camp (before the people). Joshua wanted Moses to forbid Eldad and Medad from prophesying. Moses replied, that he wished that all of God's people were prophets and that He would put His Spirit on everyone. The word prophecy in Hebrew comes from the root word "nabi", meaning to bubble forth as from a fountain. This definition points to the Holy Spirit, being the source of all prophecy. Prophecy is a spoken Word of God to man.

2nd and 3rd Witnesses

Another example is found in St. Luke chapter one, with Elisabeth and Zacharias, the parents of John the Baptist. When Mary the mother of Jesus entered Zacharias' house, Elisabeth was filled with the Holy Ghost and immediately began to prophesy. Later, Zacharias who was unable to speak before the birth of his son, was filled with the Holy Ghost and immediately began to prophesy.

The Bible says, "At the mouth of two or three witnesses, shall the matter be established."[4]   This rule concerns receiving accusations, but it is also a good general rule to use when trying to establish spiritual facts.

In these examples everyone who was filled with the Spirit prophesied rather than speaking in tongues.   That is because all of these witnesses are from the Old Testament era, even though two are from the book of Luke. Anything that precedes the resurrection of Jesus really belongs to the Old Testament dispensation.

> *Acts 2: And **when the day of Pentecost was fully come**, they were all with one accord in one place.*
> *Acts 2:2 And suddenly there came a sound from heaven as of a rushing mighty wind, and it filled all the house where they were sitting.*
> *Acts 2:3 And there appeared unto them cloven tongues like as of fire, and it sat upon each of them.*
> *Acts 2:4 **And they were all filled with the Holy Ghost, and began to speak with other tongues, as the Spirit gave them utterance.***

The first time we see anyone receive the Holy Ghost in the New Testament era, they do not prophesy, but they speak in tongues. But, what did they say in tongues?

*Acts 2:7 And they were all amazed and marvelled, saying one to another, **Behold, are not all these which speak Galilaeans?***
*Acts 2:8 And **how hear we every man in our own tongue, wherein we were born?***
Acts 2:9 Parthians, and Medes, and Elamites, and the dwellers in Mesopotamia, and in Judaea, and Cappadocia, in Pontus, and Asia,
Acts 2:10 Phrygia, and Pamphylia, in Egypt, and in the parts of Libya about Cyrene, and strangers of Rome, Jews and proselytes,
*Acts 2:11 Cretes and Arabians, **we do hear them speak in our tongues the wonderful works of God.***

All of the apostles and disciples that were present spoke about the wonderful works of God, in tongues. In other words, they all began to prophesy in different languages. Just like the 70 elders did with Moses, here 120 disciples responded to being filled with the Spirit in the same way. What is the difference between speaking in tongues and prophesying? There is no difference if the tongues are followed by an interpretation.

*1 Corinthians 14:5 I would that ye all spake with tongues, but rather that ye prophesied: **for greater is he that prophesieth than he that speaketh with tongues, except he interpret, that the church may receive edifying.***

The apostle Paul tells us that in Church, prophecy is greater than tongues, unless there is an interpretation. If the tongues are interpreted, then they are equal with prophecy. He bases this on the fact that if tongues are spoken in Church and no one interprets, what is said in tongues is meaningless to the congregation. Prophecy on the other hand is always communicated in a language that is known by the speaker and the congregation.

The scriptures clearly confirm that when someone is filled with the Holy Spirit, they speak in tongues or prophesy. This is the manifestation of the Spirit, it is the proof or evidence that the Spirit of God dwells inside of you. In fact, there are no instances in the Bible of someone being filled with the Holy Ghost without the outward manifestation of either prophecy (Old Testament) or tongues (New Testament).

Keep in mind, the infilling of the Holy Ghost is the law (Word) that God promised to write upon our hearts.[5] If we become filled with the Word via the Spirit, then naturally we will prophesy. The scriptures declare that out of the abundance of the heart the mouth speaks.[6] Speaking forth God's Word is the very definition of prophecy. This is why tongues (prophesy) is evidence of being filled with the Spirit.

Some struggle with the manifestation of the Spirit, speaking in tongues. How exactly do we get to that point? The Spirit of God fills us and then begins to communicate to us. How does the Holy Ghost speak to us? First, the Spirit of God resides inside of our human spirit. So, when He speaks, it is to our spirit. God communicates to us through His Holy Spirit, directly to our human spirit.

Our mind (soul) interprets the spiritual realm via our intuition, the sixth sense. Intuition is a knowing, a sensing that is beyond our conscious understanding, a gut feeling so to speak. All six of your senses operate in the same way. When you smell smoke, your brain does not know whether there is a fire or any real danger. But your sense of smell interacts with the brain (soul) and tries to interpret what is going on. The brain will try to employ one or more of the other senses to determine whether there is any real danger or not. The same holds true for your intuition; whenever it interacts with your brain, the mind tries to interpret what is happening. Your brain will try to employ the other senses to make a determination.

The problem is far too often we brush off what our intuition says, because we cannot find anything tangible to substantiate what we feel. It is not always possible to verify what our intuition discerns with our physical senses, but it is always a trustworthy guide.

The Holy Ghost speaks to our human spirit, it in turns communicates with our mind, through the facility of our intuition. Our conscious mind gets the impression, hunch or message and has to make a decision. Most people hesitate when starting to speak in tongues, especially men, because it is gibberish to our rational minds. We are embarrassed that we might look foolish and we resist.

The Spirit will never speak through you without your permission, which could only happen if you became possessed. The Holy Ghost does not possess or take over people, He dwells inside to lead and guide us. If you are going to speak in tongues, you will have to open your mouth and speak what you feel the Spirit is saying.

In order to begin speaking in tongues, I suggest that you start off by praising God and then just naturally flow into whatever is bubbling up (prophecy) inside through your intuition. The more you allow the Spirit to speak through you, the more comfortable you will become. After awhile it will become natural and you will do it freely and at your will.

```
┌─────────────────┐
│┌───────────────┐│
││  Chapter 4    ││
│└───────────────┘│
└─────────────────┘
```

The Need for the Holy Spirit

What lies behind us and what lies before us are tiny matters compared to what lies within us.
Ralph Waldo Emerson

In the beginning when God created man, He breathed into his nostrils and man became a living soul. Then, God planted a garden in Eden and placed the man in the garden. The man was charged to dress (cultivate) the garden and keep it. Adam was accountable to foster the growth of Eden. In other words, the garden was man's responsibility not God's. This shows the great trust and authority given to man.

> The Garden of Eden was man's responsibility not God's

There were two trees in the middle of the garden, one the Tree of Life and the other the Tree of the Knowledge of Good and Evil. Adam could eat freely from every tree in the garden, including the Tree of Life, but he could not eat from the Tree of Knowledge of Good and Evil.

> **Knowledge** - the fact or condition of being acquainted (knowing first hand) with something gained through experience or association

Before Adam ate the fruit of the Tree of Knowledge of Good and Evil, he only knew good. When man sinned, his condition changed, he gained first hand knowledge of evil. Before the fall, evil was foreign to Adam. Now, man possessed knowledge of both good and evil. Adam was immediately expelled from the garden, to prevent him from accessing the Tree of Life again and gaining eternal life.

Simply eating from the Tree of Life again would not cause Adam to live forever. God did not want man to begin to cultivate the fruit outside of the garden; if he did, man would continually eat the fruit and in doing so, live forever in bodily form, being evil.

Adam's new dual nature of good and evil gave him more than simply knowledge. It started a war inside of him. Both natures seek to influence his behavior. The problem is that they are diametrically opposed to each other and this has caused enmity between the two. In religious terminology this condition is called being a "sinner". In medical terms this state is called *Dissociative Identity Disorder* formerly *Multiple Personality Disorder*.

> **Dissociative Identity Disorder** is a psychiatric diagnosis that describes a condition in which a single human displays multiple distinct identities or personalities (known as alter egos), each with its own pattern of perceiving and interacting with the environment. The diagnosis requires that at least

two personalities routinely take control of the individual's behavior.

Instead of Adam becoming more like God, he now has a mental disorder and is in need of psychiatric care. Spiritually speaking he is a sinner in need or a Savior. Now, instead of man choosing good over evil, evil begins to control him.

> *Genesis 6:5 The LORD saw how great man's wickedness on the earth had become, and that every inclination of the thoughts of his heart was only evil all the time. (NIV)*
> *Genesis 6:6 The LORD was grieved that he had made man on the earth, and his heart was filled with pain. (NIV)*

The result of Adam's disobedience is clearly displayed in his descendants. Israel becomes our object lesson, concerning sin. The Law proves that mankind did not just make a mistake in the garden, but that they are now incapable of obeying God. The Law with its sacrifices was given to man in order that he might see himself and his need for a savior.

First, a physical or natural observance is instituted, normally an Old Testament pattern for our understanding. Afterward, the spiritual reality is established. The physical representation is temporary. It foreshadows the permanent spiritual truth.

> *1 Corinthians 15:46 Howbeit that was not first which is spiritual, but that which is natural; and afterward that which is spiritual.*

The apostle Paul summarizes the progression of the Garden of Eden saga, in the book of Ephesians chapter two. He contrasts the Gentiles to the Jews. The Law becoming a source of enmity (active and typically mutual hatred or ill will) between the two groups, one representing good, the other evil.

Knowledge of Good (God)	Knowledge of Evil (Devil)
Israelites	Gentiles
Circumcision	Uncircumcision
Nigh to God	Far off from God
Commonwealth of Israel	Aliens to Israel
Fellow citizens	Strangers
Household (family) of God	Foreigners

But, even the Law could not stop the children of Israel from suffering the effects of sin. The Law is Holy and it is from God, but it does not resolve the two natures in man. Paul stated that the Law was added because of transgressions, till Christ would come (Galatians 3:19). Everybody was concluded to be under sin, both Jews and Gentiles alike, until Christ finished His work on the cross. Jesus is God's remedy for sin.

Now that God has provided a cure for man's *Multiple Personality Disorder*, He can once again allow His Spirit to reside in man. But, how does Jesus solve our problem of dual natures? The apostle Paul posed the very same question?

> *Romans 7:18 For I know that in me (that is, in my flesh,)dwelleth no good thing: for to will is present with me; but how to perform that which is good I find not.*
> *Romans 7:19 For the good that I would I do not: but the evil which I would not, that I do.*

Romans 7:20 Now if I do that I would not, it is no more I that do it, but sin that dwelleth in me.
Romans 7:21 I find then a law, that, when I would do good, evil is present with me.
Romans 7:22 **For I delight in the law of God after the inward man:**
Romans 7:23 **But I see another law in my members, warring against the law of my mind,** *and bringing me into captivity to the law of sin which is in my members.*
Romans 7:24 **O wretched man that I am! who shall deliver me from the body of this death?**
Romans 7:25 I thank God through Jesus Christ our Lord. **So then with the mind I myself serve the law of God; but with the flesh the law of sin.**

First, the penalty for man's sin had to be paid in full. The penalty required that man would die. This is why Christ had to come in the form of a man, before He could go to the cross. Second, Jesus had to be sinless. Otherwise, He would only be paying the price for His own sins. Mankind would still be lost, because Christ would not be a true substitute if He had His own sins. Naturally speaking I could not take someone else's death penalty, if I was facing my own. It would only be a valid substitution if I was not deserving of death.

Since Jesus died for us, we are now free from the penalty of death. So, at the end of my life if I have been found guilty of sin and deserve death, Jesus' will have already paid that price for me. This is the "Good News" of the gospel. **This is why it is imperative that we share the gospel, because if you reject it, you are rejecting Christ's substitute for your death.**

If we accept Jesus' sacrifice, then spiritually we also died with Him and correspondingly we live with Him, in the heavens. This is not a physical fact, but it is a spiritual one. God and the Law consider us dead through Jesus.

After we accept Christ, we have a choice to make. We can live our lives in the physical (natural) realm or we can live in the spiritual realm. If we choose the physical realm, then we will still have the problem of two natures vying for control. If we decide to live in the spiritual realm, then we must consider ourselves (flesh) dead, but alive in Christ.

Sadly, a lot of Christians are living in the physical realm. They are what I call *Carnal Christians*. They fight constantly with their flesh and blame it on the Devil. Many believe and are taught, they are having warfare with the enemy. Believers are focusing on the Devil, when the war is internal. Jesus said, "My yoke is easy and my burden is light." So, where is the victory?

After we make the choice to accept Christ, we must decide daily what realm we are going to abide in. In order to live in the spiritual realm, we need the eyes of faith. Our physical senses are for the earth. This is why the apostle Paul said, "We walk by faith and not by sight."[7] Faith believes whole heartedly in the Word of God.

By faith we are now in heavenly places in Christ (Ephesians 2:6). By faith we reckon (consider) ourselves dead to the flesh (sin), but alive through Christ (Romans 6:11). It is through our faith that we have already overcome the world, really our flesh (1 John 5:4-5). Faith tells us that we are made in the image and likeness of the Godhead (Genesis 1:26-27), therefore we function like God functions. How does God function?

God speaks things into existence. God speaks and it is. Therefore, we speak and it is. How is this so? First, God gave man the authority through Christ. Second, God gave man the power of the Holy Ghost, to back what man says. The Spirit hastens to perform God's Word, so that it does not come back void.

In order to be effective, we need the authority of Christ and the power of the Spirit. This is akin to a police officer, who needs the authority of the badge and the power of their firearm. When an officer of the law is trying to apprehend someone, they yell, stop police. If the authority of their badge does not make you stop, the power of their weapon will.

By faith we are no longer torn between serving the law of God and the law of sin. Since we died in Christ on the cross and we rose with Him, we now serve the law of the Spirit.

There is only one law that controls the earth, reciprocity, which is sowing and reaping. This one law applies to everything. God gave Moses the commandments, to stop man from sowing evil and thereby reaping evil. This is why the soul that sins against God dies, because God is life. If you go against life, you can only get (reap) death.

Reciprocity causes us to get what we give. This is why God tells us to love our neighbor, to be merciful, not to judge others and to forgive, because the law causes us to reap it back in full. This is the reason why Jesus had to come in human form and die, because the law of reciprocity demanded it. Through sin death (separation from God) is required of every one of us.

Even when you kept the Law of Moses, as a sinner you were obligated to the law of reciprocity. Therefore, the only way man could live (be with God) was if there was a substitute for him, that did not have this obligation. Jesus then became the solution to man's great dilemma.

Jesus' death on the cross took care of separation from God. If we accept His death, then He becomes our proxy. This is what makes the gospel, good news and why it is imperative for us to spread it.

Jesus died so we no longer have to die, but the law of sowing and reaping is still in effect on earth. So, whenever I do wrong, I pay the consequence. I may not die, but I will suffer greatly, until I can live in harmony with this law. Again, the solution is Jesus. Since He substituted for us and died, we can substitute with Him and live.

Now, because of this substitution we will have everything that is Christ's. The law of this world is still reaping and sowing. How do we get around it? The only way around the law that governs this world, is to come out of it. In the heavenly realm, the law of the Spirit, which is the law of grace, governs.

The only way we could experience the law of grace in this realm, is by substitution with Christ. Since, He took the penalty of our sins, He became separated from God. This was a permanent situation. If the Father did not extend grace to Christ, then we could never experience it. Every blessing of salvation we have is because of and comes through Jesus Christ. So, in order for us to experience grace, God had to first extend it Jesus. God's grace is the reason why Jesus could rise from the grave, after only three days.

Grace means to have mercy or to pardon. By granting Jesus a pardon, we can now experience the grace that was shown to Him. Therefore, the eye for an eye justice of reciprocity no longer applies to us. Now when we sin, we can simply ask forgiveness and be pardoned because of the grace of Christ. Remember, by substitution we are living through Christ.

> *Ephesians 2:4* **But God**, *who is rich in mercy, for his great love wherewith he loved us,*
> *Ephesians 2:5* *Even when we were dead in sins,* **hath quickened us together with Christ**, *(by grace ye are saved;)*
> *Ephesians 2:6* **And hath raised us up together, and made us sit together in heavenly places in Christ Jesus:**

It is only by the Spirit of God that we have been quickened (made alive) together with Christ. Now that we live in the Spirit under the law of grace, we are no longer bound by the law of reciprocity. **Without Jesus there would be no grounds for grace and without the Spirit there would be no means to receive it.**

Every believer has been sealed with the Holy Spirit of Promise. The promise of the Spirit is that we are still waiting on God to complete our redemption. Presently, our spirits have been regenerated to house the Holy Ghost and our souls have experienced redemption from death, but our bodies are still awaiting the resurrection power of Christ.

Until then, the Adamic nature (Good and Evil) still exists within us, but thanks be to God, who has given us the victory in Christ. We must walk by faith and not by sight.

*1 John 5:4 For whatsoever is born of God overcometh the world: and **this is the victory that overcometh the world, even our faith.***

Finally, in the New Jerusalem, in the midst of the street and on both sides of the river that flows from the temple of God, there will be a tree. In this new Garden of Eden scenario, there are still two trees, but this time both are the Tree of Life. Mankind will eat freely and live forever, Jesus having eliminated the effects of Adam through the cross. The war of Good and Evil will no longer interfere with God's supreme creation, man.

Chapter 5

The Gifts of the Holy Spirit

Now there are diversities of gifts, but the same
Spirit. And there are differences of administrations,
but the same Lord. And there are diversities of
operations, but it is the same God which worketh all
in all. But the manifestation of the Spirit is given to
every man to profit withal.

1 Corinthians 12:4-7

The gifts of the Holy Spirit are given to believers for the benefit of the Church. The gifts listed in 1 Corinthians 12 are for the benefit of body of Christ, not the individual. Paul lists three distinct areas, for which the Holy Ghost supplies.

1. Gifts
2. Administrations
3. Operations

Gifts - a notable capacity, talent, or endowment

Administrations - a body of persons who oversee as in a government (Kingdom of God)

Operations – performance of a practical work, action or mission, including its planning and execution

There are nine gifts of the Spirit listed in 1 Corinthians 12. I will address the gifts in the order listed. The gifts however are given as the Spirit desires. **Every believer does not have one of the nine gifts, but they do have the manifestation of the Spirit.**

A manifestation is a perceptible, outward, or visible expression or a public demonstration of power and purpose. The Holy Spirit's transforming effect on our lives is the demonstration of power that is given to every believer. The gifts that Paul lists are specific to the Church, not the believer.

> *Romans 11:29 For the gifts and calling of God are without repentance.*

Everyone is given gifts and talents that come from God. The gifts are given at birth without repentance. The nine gifts listed in 1 Corinthians 12, are for the Church and do for the most part require repentance. An example of how the Holy Ghost gives us gifts that are without repentance, is found in the book of Exodus.

> *Exodus 35:30 And Moses said unto the children of Israel, **See, the LORD hath called by name Bezaleel** the son of Uri, the son of Hur, of the tribe of Judah;*
> *Exodus 35:31 **And he hath filled him with the spirit of God, in wisdom, in understanding, and in knowledge, and in all manner of workmanship;***

Exodus 35:32 And to devise curious works, to work in gold, and in silver, and in brass,
Exodus 35:33 And in the cutting of stones, to set them, and in carving of wood, to make any manner of cunning work.
Exodus 35:34 **And he hath put in his heart that he may teach, both he, and Aholiab,** *the son of Ahisamach, of the tribe of Dan.*
Exodus 35:35 **Them hath he filled with wisdom of heart, to work all manner of work, of the engraver, and of the cunning workman, and of the embroiderer, in blue, and in purple, in scarlet, and in fine linen, and of the weaver, even of them that do any work, and of those that devise cunning work.**

The gifts can be used for personal benefit, since they are given to us before we come to Christ. The primary use of the gifts that are without repentance is to glorify God, outside of the Church, but the gifts in 1 Corinthians 12 are to bring glory to God within the Church.

The gifts that Paul lists are primarily for those who serve in an administrative capacity (Apostles, Prophets, Evangelists, Pastors, etc.). These individuals normally have multiple gifts, since they have leadership roles in the Church. The gifts of "Divers Kinds of Tongues" and the "Interpretation of Tongues" are notable exceptions. These gifts are not necessarily connected to those in an administrative function.

In addition the gifts of "Faith" and the "Discernment of Spirits" are not always associated to leadership, but the ministry should have both in operation, in order to be effective.

"Diversities of Operations" within the Church is any job, function or board that is needed to help the Church run effectively. Deacons serve as a good biblical example of operations in the Church. Leaders in this area may not necessarily have any of the nine gifts listed by Paul, but they will most likely be very gifted and talented individuals.

Diversities of operations are just as critical to the Church as administrations. The Holy Ghost is the one who provides gifting for both areas and the people who fill these positions should be filled with the Spirit as a prerequisite.

Word of Wisdom:

The Word of Wisdom gives a person the ability to judge and make decisions with soundness, prudence, and intelligence as applied to a specific situation in the Church. **This gift and all gifts, works only at the discretion of the Spirit, not the individual.** An example of this gift is found in the Old Testament with King Solomon.

> *1 Kings 3:23 Then said the king, The one saith,*
> *This is my son that liveth, and thy son is the dead:*
> *and the other saith, Nay; but thy son is the dead,*
> *and my son is the living.*
> *1 Kings 3:24 And the king said, Bring me a sword.*
> *And they brought a sword before the king.*
> *1 Kings 3:25 And the king said, **Divide the living***
> ***child in two, and give half to the one, and half to***
> ***the other.***
> *1 Kings 3:26 Then spake the woman whose the*
> *living child was unto the king, for her bowels*
> *yearned upon her son, and she said, O my lord, give*
> *her the living child, and in no wise slay it. But the*

other said, Let it be neither mine nor thine, but
divide it.
1 Kings 3:27 Then the king answered and said,
Give her the living child, and in no wise slay it: she
is the mother thereof.
*1 Kings 3:28 And **all Israel heard of the judgment***
***which the king had judged**; and they feared the*
*king: for they saw that **the wisdom of God was in***
***him, to do judgment**.*

Word of Knowledge:

The Word of Knowledge is the revelation of information concerning a specific thing or event that the person would not normally have knowledge about. It would be as if they got the information firsthand, without being there. An example of this gift is found in the book of St. John with Jesus and the woman at the well.

*St. John 4:16 **Jesus saith unto her, Go, call thy***
husband, and come hither.
St. John 4:17 The woman answered and said, I
*have no husband. **Jesus said unto her, Thou hast***
well said, I have no husband:
*St. John 4:18 **For thou hast had five husbands;***
***and he whom thou now hast is not thy husband**: in*
that saidst thou truly.
*St. John 4:19 The **woman saith** unto him, Sir, **I***
***perceive that thou art a prophet**.*

Faith:

The Gift of Faith is special faith for the body of Christ. Every Christian has a measure of faith. The believer's faith is to be applied to the individual and their circumstances. **The gift of faith is for the Church and is pertains to the Church's needs.** Caleb is a great example of the gift of faith. He had faith to act for the whole congregation of Israel. This gift must be active in those who are in leadership, for the Church to function properly and the advancement of the Kingdom of God.

> *Numbers 13:30 And **Caleb stilled the people before Moses, and said, Let us go up at once, and possess it; for we are well able to overcome it.***

Gifts of Healing:

The Gifts of Healing is different than laying hands on the sick. Every believer has the authority to lay hands on the sick and the Word declares that the sick will recover. Laying on of hands is strictly by our authority. The gifts of healing do not occur by our authority, but by the power and flow of the Holy Spirit.

Notice that it is the gifts of healing, not the gift of healing. This indicates that there is more than one type of healing gift. This is why you will see that some healers seem to be more proficient at certain types of illnesses, than others. Jesus, however possessed all gifts of healing, because in Him was the fullness of the Spirit. The woman with the issue of blood is often used as an example of faith, but she also illustrates the gifts of healing that were in operation in Jesus.

> *St. Matthew 5:28 For she said, If I may touch but his clothes, I shall be whole.*

*St. Matthew 5:29 And straightway the fountain of
her blood was dried up; and she felt in her body
that she was healed of that plague.*
*St. Matthew 5:30 And **Jesus, immediately knowing
in himself that virtue [power] had gone out of him,**
turned him about in the press, and said, Who
touched my clothes?*

The woman's faith is what caused her to touch the hem of
Jesus' garments, but when she did, it was the gifts of
healing that was resident in Jesus that healed her.

Working of Miracles:

Working of Miracles is a manifestation of divine power to
perform something that could not be done naturally,
through the physical laws that we are aware of. There are
many examples of miracles throughout the Bible. Miracles
are performed in order to cause people to believe in the
power of God. The book of St. John gives us Jesus' first
recorded miracle.

*St. John 2:7 **Jesus saith unto them, Fill the
waterpots with water.** And they filled them up to the
brim.*
*St. John 2:8 **And he saith unto them, Draw out
now, and bear unto the governor of the feast.** And
they bare it.*
*St. John 2:9 **When the ruler of the feast had tasted
the water that was made wine, and knew not
whence it was:** (but the servants which drew the
water knew;) the governor of the feast called the
bridegroom,*
*St. John 2:10 And saith unto him, Every man at the
beginning doth set forth good wine; and when men*

*have well drunk, then that which is worse: but **thou hast kept the good wine until now.***
St. John 2:11 This beginning of miracles did Jesus in Cana of Galilee, and manifested forth his glory; and his disciples believed on him.

Prophecy:

Prophets were the vehicle of God to communicate His mind and will to men. Prophecy is a spoken Word of God to man. **The foretelling of future events is not a necessary, but only a minor part of this gift.** The whole Word of God is prophetic, inasmuch as it was written by men who communicated what they received from the Lord.

Everyone that has a word of prophecy is not a prophet. The prophet is someone who is set aside for administration of the Church. Prophets have several gifts of the Spirit including prophecy. However, every believer when they are filled with the Spirit has the ability to prophesy.

Everyone that has a word of prophecy is not a prophet.

Everyone should receive a Word from God and that is regarded to be a prophecy. Everyone can have a word for the Church directly from God, at one time or another. The fact that you prophesy, does not qualify you to be a prophet. For example, everyone that sings a song is not considered a singer. A singer is a professional, that is their vocation, but anybody can sing a song. Likewise, a prophet is a vocation or calling from God, but all believers can prophesy.

The "word of knowledge" is similar to gift of "prophecy" when it is observed, it is at times indistinguishable. This is because the two are usually used in conjunction with each other. The word of knowledge concerns knowledge about something specific that has occurred in the past or present. It is akin to insider information spiritually speaking. It is a fact or facts that are being revealed. A word of knowledge by itself is not prophecy. Prophecy may or may not contain a word of knowledge. A prophet will normally possess both gifts.

Jeremiah 37:6 **Then came the word of the LORD unto the prophet Jeremiah,** *saying,*
Jeremiah 37:7 Thus saith the LORD, the God of Israel; Thus shall ye say to the king of Judah, that sent you unto me to enquire of me; Behold, Pharaoh's army, which is come forth to help you, shall return to Egypt into their own land.
Jeremiah 37:8 And the Chaldeans shall come again, and fight against this city, and take it, and burn it with fire.
Jeremiah 37:9 Thus saith the LORD; Deceive not yourselves, saying, The Chaldeans shall surely depart from us: for they shall not depart.
Jeremiah 37:10 For though ye had smitten the whole army of the Chaldeans that fight against you, and there remained but wounded men among them, yet should they rise up every man in his tent, and burn this city with fire.

Discerning of Spirits:

Discerning of Spirits is to detect the true spirit behind the acts and manifestations taking place around us. People who have this gift can see into the spirit realm, in other words they can see the real you. There is no hiding or cloaking your intentions, when this gift is in operation. Those who have this gift can see into the past, present and future.

If you are going to make people intercessors in your Church, make sure at the least, the lead people have the gift of discernment. These are your watchmen on the wall. They see the enemy before he comes and should sound the alarm. Individuals without the gift of discernment can be intercessors, but they will need to know what to pray about.

> People who have the gift of discernment should be the primary intercessors in your Church. These are your watchmen on the wall.

St. Mark 2:6 But there were certain of the scribes sitting there, and reasoning in their hearts,
St. Mark 2:7 Why doth this man thus speak blasphemies? who can forgive sins but God only?
*St. Mark 2:8 And **immediately when Jesus perceived in his spirit that they so reasoned within themselves,** he said unto them, Why reason ye these things in your hearts?*
St. Mark 2:9 Whether is it easier to say to the sick of the palsy, Thy sins be forgiven thee; or to say, Arise, and take up thy bed, and walk?

Divers Kinds of Tongues:

Divers (diverse) kinds of Tongues are prophesying in a different language from the speaker's language or languages. Divers kinds of tongues are different than speaking in tongues. The former is for the Church and the latter is for personal use.

Every Spirit filled believer has the ability to speak in tongues. This does not mean that everyone should speak out loud during a Church service. A person should only speak out loud during the service when the Spirit is prompting them to prophesy in tongues. Otherwise, they should speak in a tone that does not disrupt the service.

If you feel prompted to speak out loud in tongues and it has been proven that there is no one to interpret, then you are to remain silent. Divers Tongues are of no use in the Church if there is no interpretation, it is just noise according to Paul.[8] Tongues as well as every other gift of the Holy Ghost can be misused or used for our own glory (ego boosting). Remember, the spirit of the prophet, is subject to the prophet. Most often with tongues the real problem is lack of understanding.

Every gift of the Holy Ghost can be misused or used for our own glory, which is ego boosting. The gifts should always bring glory (attention) to God, not us.

There are three hard and fast rules, for using Divers Kinds of Tongues in Church. As with all things, you are subject to the leadership of your own Church. Remember, obedience is better than sacrifice.

1. Make sure the Spirit is prompting you to speak to the whole Church
2. Insure that someone is present to interpret (1 Corinthians 14:28)
3. Have no more than three occurrences of Tongues during a service (1 Corinthians 14:27)

Divers tongues with interpretation are for the benefit of the Church,[9] but speaking in tongues is for the individual believer's edification.[10] The public use of tongues is a word from God, but the private use of tongues is used to speak to the Lord. The apostle said that he spoke in tongues (the private gifting) more than anyone in the assembly, but in the Church he rarely used tongues (the public gifting). Paul urged us to understand the purpose and need for the gift and to use wisdom (1 Corinthians 14:18-20).

> Divers tongues is a public gift that speaks to the Church, but speaking in tongues is a private gift used to communicate to God

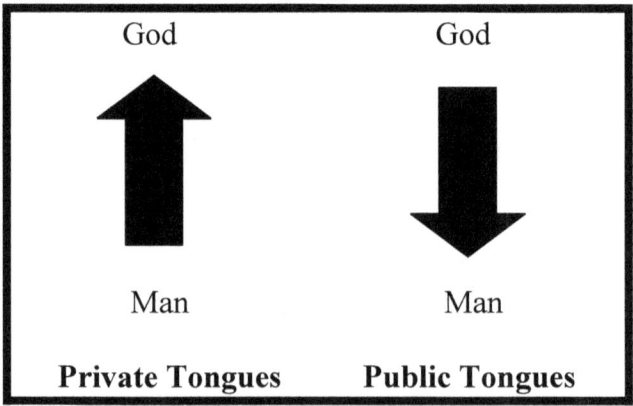

God	God
↑	↓
Man	Man
Private Tongues	**Public Tongues**

The book of Acts shows us a perfect example of Divers kinds of Tongues. On the day of Pentecost the disciples prophesied in tongues about the wonderful works of God. The gift of interpretation was not needed, because the unbelievers understood what was being said.

> *Acts 2:4* ***And they were all filled with the Holy Ghost, and began to speak with other tongues, as the Spirit gave them utterance.***

Acts 2:7 And they were all amazed and marvelled, saying one to another, Behold, are not all these which speak Galilaeans?
*Acts 2:8 And **how hear we every man in our own tongue, wherein we were born?***
Acts 2:9 Parthians, and Medes, and Elamites, and the dwellers in Mesopotamia, and in Judaea, and Cappadocia, in Pontus, and Asia,
Acts 2:10 Phrygia, and Pamphylia, in Egypt, and in the parts of Libya about Cyrene, and strangers of Rome, Jews and proselytes,
*Acts 2:11 Cretes and Arabians, **we do hear them speak in our tongues the wonderful works of God.***

The use of tongues both public and private is not always words of a human dialect. Tongues can also be groanings, which are unintelligible or non-understandable utterances.

*Romans 8:26 Likewise the Spirit also helpeth our infirmities: for we know not what we should pray for as we ought: **but the Spirit itself maketh intercession for us with groanings which cannot be uttered.***

The New International Version of the Bible makes it a little more understandable to modern readers.

*Romans 8:26 In the same way, the Spirit helps us in our weakness. We do not know what we ought to pray for, **but the Spirit himself intercedes for us with groans that words cannot express.***

Our language and words are limited to what we know and understand as humans. Spiritually there are things that we do not humanly understand and therefore have no words to express ourselves. This is why the Spirit must intercede for us, with words unintelligible to us. Some in the Church aptly call these utterances our heavenly language.

Interpretation of Tongues:

Interpretation of tongues is translating the message of divers kinds of tongues, so that the prophecy may be understood by everyone. It is not necessary to interpret when you are speaking in tongues (private gift), because you are communicating to God via the Spirit. It is only when God is speaking to us that it is imperative to have understanding.

The interpretation of tongues is straightforward and there are no biblical examples given to us. This gift is somewhat subjective, in the fact that no one can speak against the interpretation, if no one can understand what is being said. This is where your prophets or those who have the gift of discernment come in, they should be able to judge the situation and tell the Church if the word is from God or not.

> *1 Corinthians 14:29* **Let the prophets speak two or three, and let the other judge.**
> *1 Corinthians 14:30 If any thing be revealed to another that sitteth by, let the first hold his peace.*
> *1 Corinthians 14:31 For ye may all prophesy one by one, that all may learn, and all may be comforted.*
> *1 Corinthians 14:32 And the spirits of the prophets are subject to the prophets.*
> *1 Corinthians 14:33* **For God is not the author of confusion, but of peace, as in all churches of the saints**.

This is not to say that every interpretation needs to be verified by a prophet before being accepted, but questionable interpretations should. If there is no one around to verify an interpretation, the Spirit of Truth in you verifies. If you disagree with an interpretation, there is protocol to follow. In Church everything should be done decently and in order, as is fitting of saints of God.

Paul closes the chapter by exhorting us to covet earnestly the best gifts and yet he will show us a better way.[11] Sandwiched in the middle of his teaching on spiritual gifts, is a chapter on love. If we eliminated 1 Corinthians 13, chapters 12 and 14 would flow seamlessly. But, as important and dynamic as the gifts are love is far more vital to the Church and the Kingdom of God.

The Gifts are temporary, but love is eternal. The gifts work from the outside in, but love works from the inside out. Only love can touch and change the hearts of people. Of all the gifts and miracles that Jesus displayed while on the earth, only love was able to save us. **The main focus of the Church and every believer should be on love, not the gifts, not the vision and not even the anointing.**

Chapter 6

The Fruit of the Spirit

But the fruit of the Spirit is love, joy, peace,
longsuffering, gentleness, goodness, faith,
Meekness, temperance: against such there is no
law.

Galatians 5:22-23

Almost everyone is familiar with at least some of the fruit of the Spirit. In Galatians chapter five, the apostle Paul draws a contrast between fruit which is produced effortlessly and work which takes our strength and effort.

Fruits are the means by which flowering plants disseminate seeds. This scattering is achieved by animals (people), wind, water, or explosive dehiscence. Explosive dehiscence is a violent shaking of the plant from an outside source, resulting in seed dispersal far from the parent plant.

The seeds of faith are dispersed from the fruit of the Spirit just like natural fruit. The seeds of course are for reproduction.

1. **People** (Animals) – as others experience God in you they inadvertently plant the seeds within themselves
2. **Holy Spirit** (Wind) – the Holy Ghost through our works and prayers plants the seeds in the hearts of people
3. **Tribulations** (Explosive Dehiscence) – the trials of life shake us and if we allow Christ to shine forth, then the seeds get scattered to those who see how we go through

Notice that it is the fruit of the Spirit, not the fruits. So, there are not nine different fruits, but one fruit that comprises love, joy, peace, etc. Fruit is naturally produced, it requires no effort on our part. Therefore, the fruit will never be lacking in any element.

Love:

First we should define what we mean by the word love, since it is so common in our language. Generally speaking when we refer to love we are talking about one of three meanings.

> **Agape** – often termed as the God kind of love
> **Eros** – is passionate love, this is where derive the word erotic
> **Philia** - means friendship or brotherly, this is where we derive the word Philadelphia

The Bible commands us to love, even as Christ loved us. This is the agape type of love, the God kind of love. What does this really mean? Love to most people is a warm feeling in the pit of your stomach. It is impossible to legislate a feeling. **Agape love simply means to value.**

God commands us to value each other, just like Christ valued us. Some people will naturally rub you the wrong way. You will meet people who you genuinely do not like, but you can still value (love) them.

Is there a difference between being commanded to love and our producing the fruit of love? The Greek word agape is used in both instances. The difference is when we are commanded to love, we are making a conscience decision to value others, but the fruit of love comes out of us naturally, we do not have to think about it. This takes time, a tree does not produce fruit overnight and it must be cultivated.

Our objective as Christians is that we love everyone spontaneously and naturally through the Spirit, not out of compulsion to the command. This comes through the transformation of the Holy Spirit, as we walk in obedience to God's Word.

Joy:

Another natural part of the indwelling of the Spirit is joy. Joy is an emotion evoked by well being, success, good fortune or by the prospect of possessing what one desires. In other words, joy is the result of our faith in God. As we grow in our Christian walk, it is unnatural for us not to have joy.

We will always have problems and unpleasant circumstances that confront us, but our confidence in God produces joy in us. We are not moved by what we see, because we walk by faith. Since joy is an emotion, we transmit it wherever we go. People begin to feel better in our presence and want to know the source of our joy. By radiating joy we share the gospel (good news) with others.

Peace:

What is peace? This is another overused word in the English language. I think we misunderstand the spiritual use of the term. As with most words there are multiple definitions, depending on its usage. **The peace that God gives us is freedom from disquieting or oppressive thoughts or emotions.**

We experience true peace only when we pull down the strongholds, cast down imaginations and bring every thought into captivity to the obedience of Christ.[12] How do we accomplish this feat? We can only do this by using the *Armor of God* listed in Ephesians 6:13-17. The peace of God will only come to us, if we win the war inside of us, the battle of good versus evil.

Armor of God
1. Belt of Truth
2. Breastplate of Righteousness
3. Boots of Peace
4. Shield of Faith
5. Helmet of Salvation
6. Sword of the Spirit

If you look carefully at every piece of the armor, you will notice that the sword of the Spirit (Word of God) is the only offensive weapon listed. Everything else is purely for defensive measures. You cannot pull down, cast down or bring anything into captivity, in a defensive posture.

Only the Word of God will pull down strongholds (smoking, drinking, etc) in your life, cast down imaginations (built up negative images of yourself) and bring your every thought into captivity, so that you can live in obedience to Christ. To accomplish this we must quote or declare the Word over our lives.

> Only the Word will pull down strongholds, cast down imaginations and bring our thoughts into captivity to the obedience to Christ

For example, every time you face a difficult circumstance or you feel overwhelmed, declare, "I am not moved by what I see because I walk by faith and not by sight". This will smash fear and doubt in your life.

Christ has already assured us the victory. He has given us the authority of God's Word and the power of the Holy Ghost within will accomplish whatever we send the Word to do. This is how the Spirit produces peace in our lives.

Longsuffering:

Longsuffering is a word we do not use much anymore, it means to patiently endure lasting offenses or hardships. Why do we need this if we can move mountains with our faith? Even with our faith we need to have longsuffering in two areas of our life. We need to be patient in our tribulations and in our dealings with others.

Jesus told us, "In this world we will have tribulation, but to be of good cheer, because He has already overcome the world."[13] Therefore, it is a given that we will have troubles in this life, due to our allegiance with Christ. Having an alliance with the world makes you an enemy of God and vice versa. [14]

The Word coupled with our faith, works one hundred percent of the time, but that does not mean the results will be instantaneous. It is at these times that our tribulations produce the patience (longsuffering), experience and hope that Paul talks about in Romans chapter five.

The second reason we need the Spirit to produce longsuffering in us, is in our dealings with others. In life we will be forced to deal with difficult people, if we are longsuffering with them, it is a testimony to Christ in us. If we lose our patience with those we find difficult, then we damage our testimony and our ability to draw others to the faith.

> *1 Timothy 1:16 Howbeit for this cause I obtained*
> *mercy, that in me first Jesus Christ might* ***shew***
> ***forth all longsuffering, for a pattern to them which***
> ***should hereafter believe on him to life everlasting.***

Gentleness:

The Holy Ghost produces the fruit of gentleness in us. When we display gentleness, it means that we are mild in our mannerisms or disposition. Mildness is the opposite of being a fanatic. The Spirit will make you strong, but not rigid in your faith. We become easy to deal with and good to be around, this is what the book of James calls wisdom (James 3:17).

Without the fruit of gentleness, how can we draw others to Christ? We do not have to try to be gentle, as the Holy

Spirit transforms us, He will produce gentleness in us.

Goodness:

The fruit of goodness does not turn us into a *Goody Two-Shoes*. Goodness is described as the nutritious, flavorful, or beneficial part of something. We through the Spirit become flavorful and beneficial to the world. Jesus put it this way, "Ye are the salt of the earth."[15]

Life can be hard. As Spirit led believers we are to make life palatable. Christians are supposed to show that there is a better way and that way is Christ. When pressed on every side and bombarded with the stresses of life, this is when believers show what is really in them. Squeeze an orange and you get orange juice, squeeze a lemon and you get lemon juice. Squeeze a believer and you should get love, joy, peace, longsuffering, gentleness, goodness, faith, meekness and temperance. There is much truth in the saying, "only what's in you will come out of you."

Faith:

Is there a difference in the fruit of faith and faith? The only difference is in the word's usage. Faith is belief combined with action. Faith as a fruit of the Spirit is confidence in God. Faith takes work on our part, but the fruit of faith occurs naturally and takes no effort from us.

Faith = Belief + Action

As we grow in Christ, we will naturally become more and more confident in the things of God, this is the fruit of faith. Others will be drawn by our confidence in the Lord and provide us with opportunities to present the gospel message.

Meekness:

Jesus is often referred to as being meek and mild. Meekness is defined as enduring injury with patience and without resentment. It has nothing to do with being timid or weak. Jesus was neither of these things, but He is often portrayed as such. Never speaking too much above a whisper, dispensing wisdom freely like a free-spirited guru that would never hurt a fly.

> Message to men: Meekness has nothing to do with being timid or weak

As far as I can derive from the scriptural accounts of Christ, He was a man's man. The Pharisees and Herodians, who were the religious leaders of that time, had this to say about him, "Master, we know that thou art true, and carest for no man: for thou regardest not the person of men." This is hardly the description of a timid or weak person.

Jesus endured injury with patience and without resentment. This is what made Him meek. Christ never held a grudge. He never sought revenge on His enemies. This is the trait that the Spirit seeks to produce in us. As we grow and begin to see what people do to us is not personal. In addition we learn not to take ourselves so seriously.

Meekness allows us to still see the good in others, after they do us wrong. We continue to fast, pray and help others in spite of what they have done. This is what the fruit of meekness is all about. It makes us more Christ like.

Temperance:

Temperance helps us to restrain and control over indulging our appetites and passions. **The blessings of the Lord make us rich and add no sorrow, but that does not mean we can continually heap things for ourselves.** We are blessed to be a blessing to others. The Spirit stops us from going to excess with things, because this becomes a stumblingblock to others, which is sin.

> *1 Corinthians 8:9 But take heed lest by any means this liberty of yours become a stumblingblock to them that are weak.*

Even in the blessings of God we need to be on watch concerning our testimony. All of the fruit of the Spirit is for the benefit of others, not us. The fruit attracts people to us, allowing them to see God in and through us. A believer's life is meant to serve as proof of God. The outgrowth of the Spirit in our lives is produced so others can taste and see that the Lord is good.

> A believer's life is meant to serve as proof of God.

Chapter 7

Walking in the Spirit

This I say then, Walk in the Spirit, and ye shall not
fulfil the lust of the flesh.

Galatians 5:25

The apostle Paul admonishes us to walk in the Spirit and we will not fulfill the lust of the flesh. How many of us do not fulfill the lust of the flesh (sin)? So, naturally the question becomes how do we walk in the Spirit?

In order to walk in the Spirit realm, we need walk by faith. The two terms are synonymous. We have been taught seeing is believing. As a result we are naturally resistant to the concept of faith, because if we cannot see it, it is extremely hard for us to believe it.

Faith goes against everything that we have been instructed to do as adults. This is why Jesus said that we must enter the Kingdom as little children.[16] Faith is not a hard concept to live by. The problem is that in order to live by faith, we must unlearn most of what we have been taught.

Living by our faith, feels like we are being foolish. We have been taught to think things through and listen to our heads not our hearts. But, God has placed His Word in our hearts.

> *Hebrews 8:10 For this is the covenant that I will make with the house of Israel after those days, saith the Lord; **I will put my laws into their mind, and write them in their hearts**: and I will be to them a God, and they shall be to me a people:*

> *2 Corinthians 3:3 Forasmuch as ye are manifestly declared to be **the epistle of Christ** ministered by us, **written not with ink, but with the Spirit of the living God;** not in tables of stone, but **in fleshy tables of the heart.***

There are three things we need to do in order to walk in the Spirit.

1. Renew our minds with the Word
2. Speak the Word
3. Follow the Spirit

Renew our Minds:

Our thoughts are the accumulation of wisdom we have collected in a fallen state. This is why we must renew our minds, through the Word. It is imperative that we read, study and meditate on the Holy scriptures. This is an important piece, because the Word produces faith.

To meditate implies a definite focusing of one's thoughts on something so as to understand it deeply. It also means to ponder (to weigh) or mutter (repeat to yourself). When we meditate on the Word, it becomes implanted in our subconscious.

The conscious mind is where we form our logical conclusions. Our conscious mind accepts God and His Laws. It is rational to us that we are spiritual beings, created in His image. We can openly acknowledge that we walk by faith and not by sight. Unfortunately, all of our actions are not based on our conscious brain.

We can know that God's Word says, "We are fearfully and wonderfully made." But, if we unconsciously have a poor self image, we will not act like the King's kid, no matter how well we know the scriptures.

We need to replace every negative and unproductive thought (image), with what the Word says about us. This is why the scriptures tell us to think, ponder or meditate on good things.

> *Philippians 4:8 Finally, brethren, **whatsoever
> things are true**, whatsoever things are **honest**,
> whatsoever things are **just**, whatsoever things are
> **pure**, whatsoever things are **lovely**, whatsoever
> things are of **good report**; if there be **any virtue**,
> and if there be **any praise**, **think on these things**.*

Once you begin to know and understand the Word of God, you need to start using it in your life. The Word will produce faith, but faith without works (action) is dead.

Speak the Word:

God speaks things into existence, Genesis chapter one is full of examples. God speaks and it is. Therefore, we speak and it is. Does that sound impossible? Is it a little bit more than we should try to take on?

> *Proverbs 18:21* **Death and life are in the power of the tongue:** *and they that love it shall eat the fruit thereof.*

Remember back in Genesis, God gave man total ownership of the Garden of Eden. More than that, God gave man dominion over everything that He created.

> *Genesis 1:26 And* **God said,** *Let us make man in our image, after our likeness: and* **let them have dominion over the fish of the sea, and over the fowl of the air, and over the cattle, and over all the earth, and over every creeping thing that creepeth upon the earth.**
> *Genesis 1:27 So God created man in his own image, in the image of God created he him; male and female created he them.*
> *Genesis 1:28 And God blessed them, and* **God said unto them, Be fruitful, and multiply, and replenish the earth, and subdue it: and have dominion over the fish of the sea, and over the fowl of the air, and over every living thing that moveth upon the earth.**

Jesus came to restore what man lost through sin. He came to heal mankind from the effects of sin (his nature of good and evil). Since we have the Spirit of Life, God's nature in us, He can freely give us all things. The Father gave us the Kingdom of God and the keys through Jesus (St. Luke 12:32, St. Matthew 16:19). If you do not believe this fact, then you are living beneath your privilege. Jesus said, "It was the Father's good pleasure to give us the Kingdom."[17]

Speak the Word of God and declare it over yourself, your family and your situations. The Word is powerful and sharper than any two edged sword. The Word of God formed the world and framed the heavens. Do you think it will not work for you? It is not about you. God said that He hastens (rushes) to perform His Word and the He honors His Word above His name (reputation). Then, God tops it off and states that His Word will not come back to Him void (empty) but it will accomplish what He sent it to do (Isaiah 55:11).

> *Deuteronomy 30:14 But **the word is very nigh unto thee, in thy mouth**, and in thy heart, that thou mayest do it.*
> *Deuteronomy 30:15 **See, I have set before thee this day life and good, and death and evil;***

Through Deuteronomy we see that we can speak words of life (good) or death (evil). Remember, we have the Spirit of Life in us, God's nature. Christ has given us His authority over every situation and we have the power of the Holy Ghost resident inside of us, this is why we can have what we say. We do not have to beg and plead with God, but we boldly make our declarations in faith. It is the law of reciprocity (sowing and reaping) in action. This is the universal law of life, some call it Karma. It does not matter what you call it, what matters is that we learn to work with it.

Whatever we sow whether good or bad, will come back to us. To sow means to plant, to introduce into a selected environment or to set in motion. So, we sow (set things in motion) by our actions, our thoughts and our words. If you want specific results, your actions, thoughts and words must all harmonize. Otherwise, the outcome will be unpredictable.

If you want specific results your actions, thoughts and words must all harmonize

We can control our actions and also our words, but in general our thoughts are random and uncontrollable. How do we get them in sync? This is where the Christian's fight begins. Here is the real battle. This is where we must be vigilant, with the words that come out of our mouths.

Words

Aligned

Rightly

Every random thought must be checked to see if it is good. If your thoughts are not things that are true (spiritually), honest (upright), just, pure, lovely, of good report, virtuous or praise worthy, then you need to speak against them. Every rightly (conforming to fact or truth rather than mere absence of error) spoken word will neutralize negative thoughts.

Only the Word of God can pull down strongholds, cast down imaginations and bring your every thought into captivity. Jesus gave us the keys to the Kingdom, which is our authority in the earth. We assert our authority by speaking the Word over our lives, families and circumstances.

Understand that both fear and faith act as magnets in your subconscious mind. This is where strongholds and imaginations reside. Your conscious mind is rational, strongholds and imaginations rarely stem from rational beliefs. We must actively replace every negative image and belief, with what God says we are. This is what the Bible means when it says, be transformed by the renewing our minds.[18] **We transform our minds by declaring the Word and meditating on it.**

Notice, Jesus never instructed us to fight, battle or to go to war with the Devil. The real fight is inside of us. If you never master yourself through the Word, you are no threat to Satan, but you are a definite stumbling block to the Kingdom of God.

> Jesus never instructed us to fight, battle or to go to war with the Devil

Your words are powerful towards yourself and your personal circumstances, but they are limited when it comes to other people. Why? If God allowed our words to greatly affect others, then imagine the harm we would do with our careless words and gossip. Truly, God is wise.

Follow the Spirit:

Our souls interpret the spiritual realm via our intuition (the sixth sense). Even so, our soul/mind needs to interpret what the intuition is trying to communicate. The mind uses the Word of God to reference what it receives from the Spirit. This is why it is imperative that we have the Word in us. As we walk in obedience to the Word, we have valid experiences for the soul to extract and interpret (1 Corinthians 2:10–14).

We have the mind of Christ through the Holy Spirit (1 Corinthians 2:16), but this relationship is spirit (ours) to Spirit (God's). Our mind will be unfruitful until we can discern what the Spirit is telling us. Your brain (soul) will begin to search for any references (the Word) or personal experiences it can relate to the Spirit's promptings. If you have references that match up to the Word of God, you will have clarity. Otherwise, you will either come up with erroneous conclusions or simply will not understand what the promptings are about. If we do not keep the Word in our hearts (mind) and walk in obedience, then we will not understand all God wants to speak to us through His Spirit.

The indwelling Holy Ghost gives us the privilege to commune with God on a daily basis, just like Adam in the garden, but with one noticeable difference—now the Lord is within us, not outside of us. Therefore, we should have the confidence to do all things because He is always with us (Hebrews 13:5–6). This is why the Bible says, that we do not need anyone to teach us.

> *1 John 2:27 But **the anointing** which ye have received of him **abideth in you, and ye need not that any man teach you**: but as the same anointing teacheth you of all things, and is truth, and is no lie, and even as it hath taught you, ye shall abide in him.*

This does not mean that we do not need teachers within the Church. It is means that in our everyday lives we have a reliable guide and spiritual advisor. We cannot error if we listen to the Spirit. Before the day of Pentecost people had to go to the prophet or someone who could get a word from God. Now we have His Spirit and God speaks directly to us, but we must trust and listen.

How do you know when it is the Holy Ghost speaking or just ourselves? I struggled with this question too long in my own life. The answer is you will not know the difference most of the time, you must trust your intuition. Remember, God has put His laws in our minds and written them in our hearts, through His Spirit. We have been reborn and are new creatures.

We can trust our intuition as a guide. **As a safeguard we need to check what you sense in your spirit and make sure it lines up with the Word of God.** If not, then it is definitely not from the Lord. As long as what you perceive does not conflict with the Bible and it is not something that is intrinsically wrong, then follow your heart.

If you are like me you want a certain feeling when the Holy Ghost is speaking. You want to know what you should pay attention to and what to ignore, because a lot of thoughts go through your mind. But, we must realize that we are spiritual beings, so the Spirit in us is a natural thing.

When God speaks to us, it is just as innate as our own thoughts. That is hard for some of us to accept, but God intends for our relationship to be natural, not spooky or super spiritual. It was normal for Adam to talk with God in the garden. It was unnatural to separate from Him. This is the relationship that Jesus has restored in us, via the Holy Ghost. We must accept it by faith, if we are to live as God intends for us. If we follow our heart, as the Spirit prompts us, we will not fulfill the lusts to the flesh. This is walking in the Spirit.

We were created in the image and likeness of God or the Godhead. God is our Father and not just our creator. Jesus has entrusted us to finish the work He started. We are accountable to build the Kingdom, here on earth. This shows the great trust and authority given to us as believers.

I encourage you today to recognize and unleash the full power of the Holy Ghost. Be determined to live a life that demonstrates the perfect will of God. If we walk in the Spirit, using His gifts and producing His fruit, then everyone will know what lies within.

Robert

Your brother in Christ

About the Author

Robert R. Davis has served in a variety of ministries as a deacon, teacher, youth director and minister, for over twenty years. He currently serves as the Assistant Pastor of New Life Worship Center in West Haven, Connecticut. He is a gifted teacher of the Word, dedicated to pursuing and sharing the full knowledge of Christ. Robert and his wife Yvette live in Connecticut with their four children, where he continues to teach, write, and study the Word of God.

In addition to this work Robert Davis has written "The Final Message (Understanding the Book of Revelation)" and "6 Things Every Christians Should Know (The Fundamentals of Christianity)".

Other books written by Robert Davis:

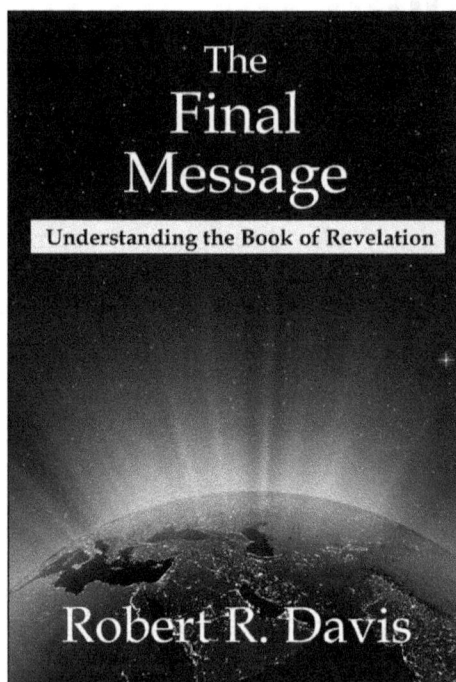

The
**Final
Message**
Understanding the Book of Revelation
Robert R. Davis

ISBN: 987-0-9797469-0-1

What makes *The Final Message* any different from the hundreds of books before it? Most books on Revelation rehash traditional interpretations with only slight variations. This work checks every vision and theory against the Bible. The Holy Scriptures are the barometer to determine whether the findings are fact or fiction. Any interpretation that cannot be verified through scripture will be disallowed, no matter how long it has been revered. Every vision is scrutinized against the rest of the Bible in order to glean its true meaning. The result is an interpretation that harmonizes perfectly with the whole Bible. You will walk away wondering why you did not see these truths before.

Other books written by Robert Davis:

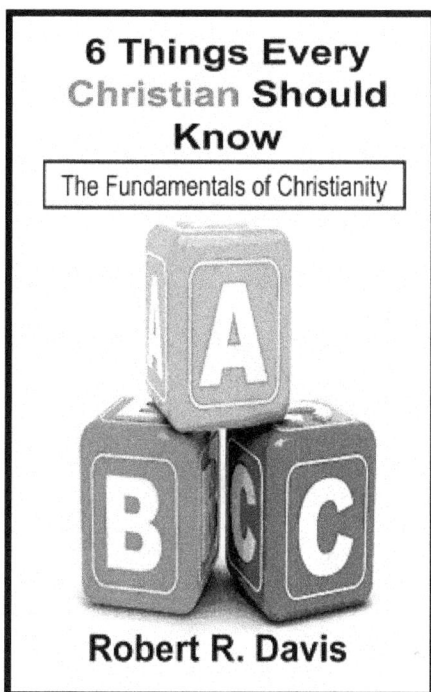

6 Things Every Christian Should Know

The Fundamentals of Christianity

Robert R. Davis

ISBN: 987-0-9797469-3-2

The book of Hebrews chapter six is the basis for this work. In it, the apostle Paul outlined what he considered the foundational truths every Christian should know. Therefore, these teachings should be the first lessons a new believer receives in the Church. Unfortunately, most Christians never receive this fundamental instruction and so attempt to build their faith without a proper foundation.

This book will not only tell you the meaning of these principles, but it explains how and why they are tied together. Insightful, fresh and reverent, it is a must have for every believer.

References:

[1] Holy Bible. St. John 14:9 (NIV).
[2] Holy Spirit (Gender of the Holy Spirit).
http://en.wikipedia.org/wiki/Holy_Spirit#cite_note-cathex-27#cite_note-cathex-27.
[3] Holy Bible. St. Matthew 28:20.
[4] Holy Bible. 2 Corinthians 13:1.
[5] Holy Bible. Hebrews 8:10.
[6] Holy Bible. St. Matthew 12:34.
[7] Holy Bible. 2 Corinthians 5:7.
[8] Holy Bible. 1 Corinthians 14:8-9.
[9] Holy Bible. 1 Corinthians 14:5.
[10] Holy Bible. 1 Corinthians 14:4.
[11] Holy Bible. 1 Corinthians 12:31.
[12] Holy Bible. 2 Corinthians 10:4-5.
[13] Holy Bible. St. John 16:33.
[14] Holy Bible. James 4:4.
[15] Holy Bible. St. Matthew 5:15.
[16] Holy Bible. St. Mark 10:15.
[17] Holy Bible. St. Luke 12:32.
[18] Holy Bible. Romans 12:2

www.ingramcontent.com/pod-product-compliance
Lightning Source LLC
Chambersburg PA
CBHW071842020426
42331CB00007B/1824